BOOK 1

THE MANUAL

POWER/PLEASURE/
POKER/PORK PIES

CARL BEECH WITH
ANDY FROST
AND BRYAN PILL

BIOGS

Carl

Carl is married to Karen and has two daughters. He's the leader of CVM (an international men's movement) and the founder of 'the code'. Previously a banker, church planter and senior pastor, he is convinced he is a great chef, plays the piano, loves cycling, movies and sci-fi books and caught a record-breaking catfish on the river Ebro in Spain.
Twitter @carlfbeech

Andy

Andy Frost is a surfer living in land locked London. He helps lead a local footie team; is passionate about helping the Church engage with contemporary culture; and runs the missionary organisation Share Jesus International.

Bryan

Bush Pilot, Guernseyman, Lover of one wife, Owner of one Kayak, Speaker, Father of three great youngsters, am a King's man. Have the best job in the world that part involves me in short-term flying for Mission Aviation Fellowship, and part gives me the chance to speak about this exciting mission to anyone who will listen.
Blog – Biggles Abroad
Youtube – bigglesgsy

Contents

BOOK 1

We've finally cracked it!
After being asked to write daily notes for men a number of times over the years, we've finally nailed it. So in a nutshell, here you go and let the journey begin!

It's a simple and well-proven approach. The notes are between 150–300 words long. Each day begins with a verse and ends in a prayer. It will take you no more than a few minutes to read but I hope that what you read stays in your head throughout your day. The notes are numbered rather than dated, so it's OK if you miss a day to pick it back up. If you want to study with a group of guys you can easily keep track of where you are up to or swap ideas on that particular study online (we've a Facebook page). If you want to be part of a band of brothers internationally swapping thoughts, insights and prayer requests then you can do that as well by using our new Facebook page.

In each issue, I've asked some of
my mates to contribute. In this
one, big thanks go to Andy Frost
and Bryan Pill for their insights and
thoughts. Both great guys going
after God's heart. We really hope
that the subjects from Pork Pies to
Poker speak into all of our lives and
help us stay on the narrow path!

So there it is. The Word of God
has such power to inform and
transform our lives, so let's knuckle
down and get reading.

Your brother in Christ
Carl

[POWER]

01/ Who's the daddy?

'In the beginning, God created the heavens and the earth. Now the earth was formless and empty, darkness was over the surface of the deep, and the Spirit of God was hovering over the waters. And God said, "Let there be light," and there was light.' **Genesis 1:1-3**

When I worked as part of the sales force in a bank, it was all about who had the nicest pen set, the best office and the most sales. When I go to the gym it all seems to be about who has the best car in the car park. When guys meet up, the first thing they ask each other is 'What do you do for a living?' I suspect that's because we are behaving like pack animals, working out the hierarchy based on who has the most influence or the biggest pay packet.

As followers of Jesus we don't play those games, do we? We already know who really has all the power and all the glory. Someone with a nice office pales into insignificance next to the God who turned on the lights of the universe.

Keep your head today – and your perspective. No matter who you are or what you do, remember we are all God's sons and that's amazing. It's His grace that allows you to live and breathe.

PRAYER: I acknowledge that all the power and the glory is with You, God. Thank You for Your grace and Your patience with me. Help me today to keep my life in perspective to Your glory. Amen.

02/A son

'The Spirit you received brought about your adoption to sonship. And by him we cry, "*Abba*, Father." The Spirit himself testifies with our spirit that we are God's children.'
Romans 8:15-16

Many men suffer with a disease called insecurity. We get our feelings of apparent security from how we are perceived, how successful we seem to be and whether we are popular or not. We worry constantly about what others think of us, which perpetuates our lack of fulfilment. I know because I've been there. I remember walking around years ago before a church meeting, stressed out and telling God I was rubbish. It was in that moment of darkness that I heard the Holy Spirit speak to me like this:

'Yes, that's true ... you've not been all that really.'

Talk about kicking a man when he's down!

Then came the killer blow …

'But you are My son and I love you … that's all that matters!'

Who cares how sophisticated or successful people think you are. You are a son of the Living God. Unconditionally loved and accepted. So man up, get the truth deep into your spirit and live a life free of worrying about what everyone else thinks about you!

Prayer: I reaffirm today that I am Your son and that You are my Father. Help me to see myself as You see me and not to be worried about how others view me. Amen.

03/A soldier's view

> 'For I myself am a man under
> authority, with soldiers under me.
> I tell this one, "Go", and he goes;
> and that one, "Come", and he comes.
> I say to my servant, "Do this", and
> he does it.' **Luke 7:8**

Isn't it interesting just how different Jesus' model
of power is from ours? I've often marvelled at
how, when Jesus was dying, He could have called
on legions of angels to cut Him loose and strike
His opponents down ... but He chose not to.
Jesus chose to exercise ultimate power with nails
through His wrists rather than by being as hard
as nails.

The Roman centurion in today's reading got it.
He had power to lead men into battle and to
send them to their deaths. He also had a range of
severe punishments and sanctions available to
him. Centurions, however, also led by example.
They fought beside their men and generally
suffered disproportionate casualties in battle

as they were first in and last out. They also understood the chain of command. So when this centurion met Jesus, he saw in Him One who had true authority and power and he was ready to submit to it.

Are you a man under authority or a rebel? Remember, God will only raise you up if He can see that you are prepared to submit and serve. You can't have authority unless you place yourself under it.

Prayer: Heavenly Father, help me to be the kind of servant that I know I ought to be. Deal with any offensive way in me, and lead me in the way everlasting. Amen.

04/ Meek ain't weak

'Blessed are the meek, for they will inherit the earth.' **Matthew 5:5**

Some men can pretty much journey through their whole lives without ever saying 'Will you forgive me?' But asking for forgiveness humbles you, as it puts all the power into the person you are speaking to. It's tough, and takes real courage, but that's how to truly exercise godly power and authority.

Whether you are a boss, a Dad, a boyfriend or part of a sports team you can choose to walk in humility and meekness or pride and defensiveness.

A senior executive in an investment bank once shared with me how he got really stressed out at work and verbally laid into everyone. That night he hardly slept knowing that he had grieved the Holy Spirit through his attitude and behaviour. The next day he called his whole team together and asked them to forgive him for his behaviour and for the things that he had said. Months later he told me that the team was performing better than ever and that there was a new level of honesty, team spirit and morale about the place. Not only is the kingdom way the right way, it works!

Prayer: Create in me a humble heart, willing to be first in apologising and dying to pride. Help me to model what it means to be a kingdom man. Amen.

[POWER]

05/ Honour

'Remember your leaders, who spoke the word of God to you.'
Hebrews 13:7

Moses knew it, Paul the apostle knew it and so do leaders in industry, public service, sports teams and churches the world over ... Being a leader is one tough gig! Usually, the decisions that need to be made will upset someone but often the reasons behind those decisions can't be shared with everyone. That is just one of the reasons that leading can be a lonely business. I believe that's why the Bible talks about giving leaders double honour and not making their lives more difficult than they already are! Interestingly, much is written about leadership but not a lot is written or said about 'follower-ship'.

Here are my thoughts on how to follow those who lead you well. A good discipline is to regularly find a way to 'bless' anyone who has to make decisions that affect you – such as a team captain, a parent or a boss at work. Try praying for those who lead you, accept their lead a bit more easily and don't join in with the typical 'moan and gripe about the boss' sessions that seem to take place everywhere. We are called to live by a higher standard. Let's show that we can and help make the lives of those in leadership a bit more easy.

Prayer: I pray today for all those in authority in my life. I pray for their blessing, wisdom and provision. Help them to stand strong in the face of criticism and be steadfast and full of integrity. Help me to support and honour those who lead me. Amen.

06/True greatness

'Whoever wants to become great among you must be your servant, and whoever wants to be first must be slave of all.' **Mark 10:43-44**

Josef Stalin was one of the world's greatest tyrants. A story is told that on one chilling occasion, he gathered his senior advisers around him and showed them a tiny bird that was nestling in his hands. Slowly but surely he plucked all the feathers out of its body. Astonishingly, the bird tried even harder to nestle into Stalin's hand for warmth even though he had essentially just tortured it. Stalin's lesson to his advisers was this: 'Take everything away from the people and they will still come to you for help.' That's an example of power corrupting.

As men of God, wherever we are, whatever influence we have been given, we need to use it to bring life, not control or destroy it. Think about how Jesus exercised power. He did it by being nailed to a cross and laying His life down.

So, wherever you have leadership or power, think about how you can promote people ahead of you, encourage, take a hit on behalf of others, protect and shield those who are weaker.

Prayer: Help me to lead as Jesus would lead. Help me to live a life that blesses others rather than making their lives difficult. Help me to be a man who puts the welfare of others in front of my own. Amen.

Do you wish to rise? Begin by descending. You plan a tower that will pierce the clouds? Lay first the foundation of humility.
St. AUGUSTINE

07/Love

> 'And now these three remain: faith, hope and love. But the greatest of these is love.'
>
> **1 Corinthians 13:13**

We are going to spend today thinking about the power of love. I'm not talking about a soppy, Mills-and-Boon-type love but, rather, a radical, costly one. This is the love that lays its life down and endures even when it hurts. It's this love that compels us to take a hit on behalf of others.

When songwriters think about love the lyrics can be incredibly shallow. When God talks about love He gives us the example of Hosea, a man told to keep on loving his adulterous, prostitute wife. Ultimately, God gave us Jesus – who was prepared to be brutally executed and still forgave as He was being nailed to the cross.

True power is found in unconditional love, which is a noble expression of masculinity. Ask me to show you a so-called 'real man' and I'll point you in the direction of a guy who doesn't need to posture or boast, because he's already laying his life down in the hidden places.

It's a tall order to live like that. That's why praying to become more like Jesus is far more radical than we often give credit for.

Prayer: I commit today to be a man who is meek not weak, humble not proud, kind not harsh, life-giving not life-destroying. Help me to develop the type of love that lays its life down for others. Amen.

08/Hold your tongue!

'My dear brothers and sisters, take note of this: everyone should be quick to listen, slow to speak and slow to become angry, because human anger does not produce the righteousness that God desires.'

`James 1:19-20`

Welcome to James. His book isn't just about lofty theological concepts but about putting faith into action. His practical, down-to-earth style is full of wisdom. Too often I am slow to listen, quick to speak and quick to become angry. Too often my human anger erupts into words as I air my petty frustrations. Words are powerful things; and the words I speak can easily cause hurt, pain and isolation.

James explains that the key issue is really one of listening. In this book James specifically challenges us to listen to God. How do we make sure we see things from His angle? How would our present situation look different if we allowed God to speak into it today?

If we have spent time listening to God, we are more able to put His ideals into practice, with words of healing, grace and truth. Sometimes this will mean getting angry. But rather than a human anger that solely sees the world from our viewpoint, we see things with a righteous anger that looks at an unjust world and wants to make a difference. What is God speaking to you about today?

Prayer: Father God, help me to listen before I act. May my words and my life overflow with Your agenda. Amen.

09/Active not passive

'What good is it, my brothers and sisters, if someone claims to have faith but has no deeds? Can such faith save them?' **James 2:14**

It's easy to say that we trust God ... but do we really?

We say that we trust God with our finances but sometimes our tight-fisted generosity paints a different picture. We say that we trust God with our work but our stress levels show that we only trust ourselves. We say that we trust God with our relationships but sometimes our desire to control highlights a fear to truly love.

We may say that we trust God for all things but sometimes our faith can be little more than mere good intentions. Instead, we put our faith in our abilities, our strength or our bank balance.

James is challenging us here to have an active faith – a faith in God that is reflected in our everyday actions. Real faith needs action or else it is merely wishful thinking.

Let's not just live under the tag 'Christian'. Rather let's live lives that reflect the Christ that we follow. Actively live out your faith today, trusting God in all things!

Prayer: Faithful God, show me how to trust You more. Help me to learn afresh that You have my best interests at heart. Help my faith to be more than words – let it flow through into my actions. Amen.

10/Submission

'Submit yourselves, then, to God.
Resist the devil, and he will flee
from you.' **James 4:7**

We are often very good at calling Jesus our
Saviour. We celebrate what He did for us in His
life, death and resurrection. However, I sometimes
think we struggle with calling Him Lord.

At the time of the Early Church, each Roman
citizen had to pledge allegiance to Caesar
every year with the burning of incense and the
statement 'Caesar is Lord'. The Early Christians
adapted this phrase and publicly stated: 'Jesus is
Lord'. You can imagine why they were persecuted
– they threatened the very fabric of Roman
civilisation by making Jesus their master rather
than Caesar.

What does it look like to make Jesus Lord in our
lives today?

James is writing to us in this section about humility. Making Jesus Lord is about being humbly obedient to the call Jesus has on our lives. It is about surrendering our way and submitting to His way – the call to love others, to live generously and to be holy. The latter is the challenge to resist the devil, battling the competing gods that are vying to become lord in our lives. It is when we resist temptation and humbly submit to God that the devil flees.

How will your life look this week as you humbly submit to Jesus and allow Him to be Lord of your life?

_____

Prayer: Lord God, keep me humble before You. Help me to make You Lord of my life and to resist the devil. Amen.

_____

11/Clock-watching

'Be patient, then, brothers and sisters, until the Lord's coming. See how the farmer waits for the land to yield its valuable crop, patiently waiting for the autumn and spring rains. You too, be patient and stand firm, because the Lord's coming is near.' **James 5:7-8**

We live in the tension between the now and the not yet. Jesus' death won the victory over the powers of darkness but, until He returns, we do not yet experience everything as it should be. We live in the 'not yet'.

This means that following Jesus is not easy. There will be trials to face, suffering to endure and storms to ride. And it's easy to grumble like the Israelites did in the wilderness. It's easy to lash out like Peter in the Garden of Gethsemane – or to want to give up like the prophet Elijah. But James challenges us to be patient.

The farmer waits patiently because he expects the harvest. We have a much greater hope in Jesus of a new heaven and a new earth where there will be 'no more tears' (Rev. 21:4). The problem is that it is too easy to lose perspective. We often focus on today's problems rather than the bigger picture of tomorrow's promises. In the midst of today's troubles, how will you remain patient as you hold on to the hope that Jesus offers?

Prayer: Eternal God, help me not to get lost in today's issues. Remind me of the bigger picture that I may be patient in the conversations, the choices and the challenges of today. Amen.

[TEMPTATION]

12/Phone a friend

'So we fix our eyes not on what is seen, but on what is unseen, since what is seen is temporary, but what is unseen is eternal.' **2 Corinthians 4:18**

We will now spend a few days looking at the issue of the temptations surrounding 'false pleasures'. We need to start by remembering where we need to keep our focus.

The truth of the matter is that this world, and of course our lives on this planet, are temporary and incredibly brief. We might sometimes think that we are going to go on forever but that's simply not true. It's just a fact of life that we all eventually die, so while we live in this world we need to make sure that we keep our gaze fixed firmly on eternal things. The world has a lot of stuff to throw at us and, being men with a chemical called testosterone coursing through our bodies, it's easy to get sidetracked or blindsided.

So, when the pressure bites or the temptations come thick and fast, remember to keep looking up to Jesus, the author and perfecter of our faith. And when you feel like you might just fail, pick up the phone and ask a mate to pray for you so that you 'don't get got'.

Prayer: I know, God, that my life here is temporary. So strengthen me by the power of Your Holy Spirit to keep looking up at Jesus and not at those things around me that would blunt my walk with You. Amen.

13/Wandering eyes

> 'And if your right hand causes you to stumble, cut it off and throw it away. It is better for you to lose one part of your body than for your whole body to go into hell.'
> **Matthew 5:30**

So here Jesus tells us to cut our hand off and throw it into the fire rather than sin. I don't see many people doing that these days, but we do need to take the command seriously. What this verse is urging us to do is to get brutal with temptation. The fact of the matter is that there is always an exit door to any temptation. Better, however, that you don't get to that point in the first place! When I was at Bible College we used to have the three-second rule. It was a fun way of keeping each other accountable. When we saw someone's eyes wandering to the beautiful woman walking down the road we would say 'three seconds mate!' (the idea being that after three seconds you started to sin). It wasn't a scientific fact but a fun way to combat temptation.

Pray today for the strength to resist. Why not ask a friend if you can start being accountable to one another? You can regularly check up on how each is doing with the temptations that you find particularly hard. Also, why not get some internet accountability software such as Covenant Eyes installed on your computer? Meditate on the Matthew passage above today and ask the Holy Spirit to help you keep your heart and motives pure.

Prayer: God, when I am under pressure to sin today, show me the exit door and give me the grit and courage to take it. I bring my life before You and acknowledge my weakness so that You can make me strong. Amen.

14/ Pink elephants and the presence of Jesus

'Therefore, since we are surrounded by a great cloud of witnesses, let us throw off everything that hinders and the sin that so easily entangles.'
Hebrews 12:1

So many men get themselves trapped in a cycle of addiction to pornography (in whatever shape or form) purely because they haven't got the right strategy to fight it. If I say to you right now, 'don't think about pink elephants', what do you immediately start thinking about? Pink elephants, right? If I tell you to think about Jesus and what He is doing in your life, you start to think about Jesus, right? That's why this passage in Hebrews is so important. It is a sharp reminder that we need to stop sinning. So, how do we do that? Well, keep your spiritual eyes firmly focused on Jesus and what He did for you. If you cultivate a lifestyle of thanks and gratitude to Him the 'other stuff' that you spend time tripping up over will in time fall away from you. So, before you go to work, college, the gym or whatever else you are doing today, spend a moment thinking about Jesus and what He has done for you.

Prayer: Heavenly Father, I pray that I will keep my eyes fixed firmly on Your Son Jesus. I determine to keep looking up at Him and to live a life of gratitude and thanks. Amen.

15/Heart surgery

'Above all else, guard your heart,
for everything you do flows from it.'
Proverbs 4:23

Here's the truth about indulging in false pleasures.
They're temporary and most of the time leave you
wrecked, feeling empty and racked with feelings
of guilt and shame. In addition, most guilty
pleasures (called that for a reason) are done in
secret and so you end up having to cover your
tracks by lying as well. It isn't until afterwards that
you realise you've been playing a soul-destroying
game of risk and self-destruction.

Most serious moral failures don't come out of
the blue. The truth is that most men who fall
have been playing with fire for a long time. The
odd flirtatious comment, the lingering look,
arranging to be where they shouldn't be – all
because it got their adrenalin going. Or perhaps
they just got really good at covering their tracks
on the internet ...

Proverbs 4:23 is probably one of the most important verses in the Bible and it gives us a key principle to live by. Let's pause and think for a minute about the 'law of diminishing returns'. The simple fact is, the more you pursue temporary and worldly pleasures, the less they satisfy and the further you go in your quest for pleasure. To put it bluntly, your sin and your testosterone will take you to places you don't want to go. So today keep these things firmly in mind and be honest about what that means for you. Oh, and keep looking up!

Prayer: I determine today to guard my heart. I repent now of wrong turnings I have taken or am taking right now. Thank You for the cross. Please create in me a pure heart. Amen.

16/Take captives

'We take captive every thought
to make it obedient to Christ.'
2 Corinthians 10:5b

Following on from yesterday, we are going to
look more closely at how to guard our hearts.
The Bible tells us to take every thought captive.
This is because as a man how you think within
yourself affects the condition of your heart for
good or ill. This is front-line stuff and the truth is
that we are in one almighty battle. Have no doubt
that the enemy (and we do have one) wants to
pollute your mind and blunt the presence of the
Holy Spirit in your life. Something that's helped
me over the years is to realise that the Holy Spirit
is actually very sensitive. We are told not to grieve
Him in Ephesians 4 and yet we so easily do. Take
the example of Samson. The Bible tells us that the
Holy Spirit had left him and he didn't even realise
(Judg. 16:20)!

It's scary that we may think we are doing OK,
but in reality we're grieving God. But as a wise

man once said to me, the time to start worrying is when you don't feel worried about that kind of thing anymore! So go to war with the thoughts and actions that you know are not pleasing to God. Do battle and fight hard. Determine today to be the kind of man that you know, under God, you ought to be.

Prayer: Please equip me for the fight of faith, strengthen me to run the race and fashion me into a godly man who honours Jesus and pleases the Holy Spirit. Amen.

17/Chit-chat

'Do not let any unwholesome talk come out of your mouths, but only what is helpful for building others up according to their needs, that it may benefit those who listen.'

Ephesians 4:29

It's so easy to use our words for destruction rather than to bring life. But we need to realise that the tongue has incredible power to destroy people. The old saying, 'sticks and stones may break my bones, but words will never hurt me', is utter rubbish. I've known people who have been affected for most of their lives by something that was said to them years before. One of my mates was told by a teacher a long time ago that his life would never amount to anything. Years later, in the eyes of the world he is a great success with significant wealth. Get him to talk honestly about how he feels, however, and he still looks back to that moment in his classroom. It defined who he is today – he's totally driven, mostly permanently stressed and still trying to prove his teacher wrong. I know more than a handful of people like this. The above verse makes it clear to us that if what we have to say isn't ultimately for good then we shouldn't say anything at all.

On the flip side, it never ceases to amaze me just how incredibly affirming a positive word spoken to someone can be. Us men can be so closed off to giving praise but I challenge us all today. Let more praise and encouragement come from your mouth than the alternative and enjoy looking at how people change around you.

Prayer: Guard my heart and my tongue, that I might bring life with my words and not discouragement and upset. Amen.

18/Kindness

'Be kind and compassionate to one another, forgiving each other, just as in Christ God forgave you.'
Ephesians 4:32

Kindness can sound to us guys like such a bland, weak word. It certainly isn't, though. It takes great care to notice those around you who need encouraging and building up and it takes a bit of extra time and effort to then do something about it. The kindest and most caring blokes I know have a healthy perspective on who they are as men of God. They know they owe God everything and are fully dependent on Him. Therefore they find it easy to forgive and, out of gratitude to God for His rescue of their lives, feel stirred to compassion.

Let your life be characterised by the hope you have in the gospel. This means demonstrating a radical kindness. Make time for people, be quick to forgive and go the extra mile for those in need.

If you think about the fact that Jesus died for you, that isn't too much of an ask.

True compassion and kindness can often come at great personal cost. In other words, you need to be courageous, not bland and weak, in order to exercise real kindness.

Prayer: May kindness, compassion and forgiveness be the hallmarks of my life. May people see me as a strong man who is prepared to take a hit on behalf of others. Amen.

19/Iron

> 'As iron sharpens iron, so
> one person sharpens another.'
> **Proverbs 27:17**

One thing's for certain – we're not meant to be
walking this journey on the narrow path as solo
super-soldiers. We're meant to be walking in
brotherhood. So learn to be a Proverbs 27:17 man.
Iron sharpens iron, right? Left on its own, after
lots of use, a blade goes blunt. It's not rocket
science to understand that we need each other,
so why do so many of us men not open up our
lives for accountability and regular sharpening?
Realise that you need brothers around you to
keep you sharp. Not only that, you need some
who will ask you honest, probing questions and
also be prepared to have you ask them back. This
is a real key to staying strong.

If you are reading this and feel that within your
marriage you are so strong that you don't need
anyone else, let me offer this thought: it's not just
about you but your mates as well ... and if, in the

unlikely event that the wheels come off for you, the safety net will be there. If you are not part of a group of guys who pray for each other, let me challenge you today to get into one. If you are in an accountability group, pick up the phone today and encourage the others with a word of Scripture. Start living this journey with your closest friends and fight shoulder to shoulder. Remember – it's not a solo battle out there.

Prayer: I acknowledge that I need good men around me to help me walk along the path of faith. Please strengthen and equip my brothers so that they, too, may run the race well and finish strong. Amen.

20/On guard

'The thief comes only to steal and kill and destroy; I have come that they may have life, and have it to the full.' **John 10:10**

We were created by God not just to serve Him and to make Him known but also to enjoy Him and the world in which we live. As we've already seen, there's enough 'stuff' out there to take your joy away from you. False and temporary pleasures numb our senses, and lead us down the wide path towards death. Jesus told us that the path to life is narrow. This doesn't mean that we need to be overly puritanical but it does mean that we need to make an effort.

Here are some ideas of what to try. Guard yourself against cynicism and pessimism, as they will bring you down. Spend time with people and do activities that make you laugh. This will bring richness into your life. Get involved in a cause that enables you to see beyond yourself. This will broaden your horizons and stop you looking inward. Start to appreciate the simple things in life. Be generous with your time and your money. Be quick to forgive and believe the best of people. Do these things and you won't look for pleasure in the wrong places. You will also discover an authentic, real and lasting joy that bears fruit in your life.

Prayer: I determine today before You, God, that I will be a man of hope, generosity, optimism and grace. Amen.

21/Is ignorance really bliss?

'How can a young person stay on the path of purity? By living according to your word. I seek you with all my heart; do not let me stray from your commands.'

Psalm 119:9-10

MAF pilots have a great working relationship with our engineers! On one recent trip to Uganda the chief engineer showed me some cracks on two tiny little compressor blades from inside one of our large, single-engine Cessna 208 Caravans. Almost impossible to see with the naked eye, this was potentially catastrophic. Ignorance can appear to be bliss; if the cracks had not been spotted I would have continued hauling passengers and cargo into and out of rough, short, bush airstrips, 'blissfully unaware' that these tiny cracks, which had developed slowly over time, were there. Their presence meant the engine might have failed just when I needed its maximum performance.

CAPTAIN BRYAN J. PILL

As soon as the engineer knew there were cracked blades in the engine the aircraft had to be grounded, as he knew what these tiny cracks were capable of causing. I could have protested and said that the plane was needed for another urgent flight, that MAF could not afford the repair. Even if I had tried to persuade the engineer to fix it later as it was only a few little cracks, it wouldn't have changed the situation.

No, only a fool would ignore the promptings of a chief engineer! It is amazing how we sometimes fail to sort out cracks in our lives, even after they have been shown to us. My advice for today is to ground yourself and get them sorted. It may be 'expensive' and uncomfortable, but you owe it to yourself and those around you to be fully operational so you are always ready to give of your best when the time is needed.

Prayer: Lord, please reveal to me an area of my life that is failing. Let me be brave enough to get it sorted out with Your guidance and help. Amen.

22/Afraid

'Do not be afraid; do not be discouraged. Be strong and courageous.' Joshua 10:25

There is a famous quote from the movie *The Fly*: 'Be afraid, be very afraid.' Fear has its uses – hey, who would want to leap out of a perfectly serviceable aircraft and then call it skydiving! Seriously, fear can stop you from doing foolish activities – but it can also prevent you from doing some amazing ones.

As a MAF pilot I operate small, 9- to 12-seat bush aircraft into often remote airstrips in Africa. These aircraft are often the only means by which people can get safely into some areas. Occasionally on meeting the passengers before a flight, I find one of them is extremely nervous and fearful of flying in what looks to them like a flimsy aircraft. Yet they trust what they have read or heard from friends and what they know about MAF that all will be well and, despite their fear, they climb aboard. I have also met people who have refused to fly and have either taken a far more dangerous and longer ground route or simply cancelled part of their trip.

Sometimes God calls us to face our fears and take the Word of God at face value. When challenges come your way today, stand firm. You are God's man for this moment.

Prayer: Lord Jesus, I want to take You at Your Word and not be afraid. Give me wisdom and strength to overcome discouragement and the day's challenges. Help me to be strong and inspire others also to be strong and courageous. Amen.

23/Hope in the morning

"'For I know the plans I have for you," declares the LORD, "plans to prosper you and not to harm you, plans to give you hope and a future."' **Jeremiah 29:11**

The Land Rover rattled merrily to itself as it headed to the airport. Its headlights picked out small flocks of bright-white shirts and a gaggle of children waved in the split-second recognition of seeing my white face bouncing past. Amazingly their voices carried through the window over the Land Rover's clatter, 'Ello Mzungu Mzungu' (white-man, foreigner), with no malice, as I slowly drove past in a swirling cloud of dust.

Glancing back in the mirror a thought flickered through my mind that, despite the time and the fact they were already a mile or two into their journey, the children were all seemingly spotless in the brief pre-dawn gloom. Each child was clutching their broom, a well-thumbed exercise book and the hope that education holds the key to their future. I remember a phrase from a long-forgotten poem, 'Hope is a star a constant ray that guides the traveller on the way'.

Despite the long walk, the early start and the dust the children were focused on the day's activity and remained clean, joyful, bright and full of hope. So as you prepare for the day's battles get yourself focused. Remember: you have a tremendous hope for the future; today you are a purveyor of hope and you have a story to tell. You also have a challenge to live for, so get up, get going and go to it ...

Prayer: Lord, today let me lay claim to the hope and future You have given me and, like those youngsters in the dark and gloom, help me remain clean and pure and hold firm to the promises You have given. Let me be known as a man of hope. Amen.

24/ Nail your colours

'I am still as strong today as the day Moses sent me out; I'm just as vigorous to go out to battle now as I was then.' **Joshua 14:11**

What a fantastic statement to be able to make! I wonder if we will still be able to say the same at the ripe old age of 85, as Caleb was then.

Before I became a MAF pilot, I taught chemistry and various outdoor activities in India at Hebron School. On Sundays we would go to Union Church where C.T. Studd, a cricketer of renown, used to preach. He wrote some inspiring stuff that has impacted my own life. The following is taken from Norman Grubbs' book on him – I pray it will challenge you too:

Nail the colours to the mast! That is the right thing to do, and, therefore, that is what we must do, and do it now. What colours? The colours of Christ, the work He has given us to do — the evangelization of all the unevangelized. Christ wants not nibblers *of the possible, but grabbers of the impossible, by faith in the omnipotence, fidelity, and wisdom of the Almighty Saviour Who gave the command. Is there a wall in our path? By our God we will leap over it! Are there lions and scorpions in our way? We will trample them under our feet! Does a mountain bar our progress? Saying, 'Be thou cast into the sea,' we will march on. Soldiers of Jesus! Never surrender! Nail the colours to the mast!**

Prayer: Lord, help me to be the man you have called me to be, a bold disciple, a man of renown. I cannot do it alone but You can walk me through the challenges of manhood. Lord, You are my Master and Commander. Amen.

---

* Norman Grubb, C.T. Studd, Cricketer and Pioneer (CLC, 1985).

25/Risk-taking

'Going a little farther, he fell to the ground and prayed that if possible the hour might pass from him. "*Abba*, Father," he said, "everything is possible for you. Take this cup from me. Yet not what I will, but what you will."' `Mark 14:35-36`

God is a risk-taker. In order for Jesus to pay the ultimate price for our sin He had to have a free choice as to whether He went to the cross or not. That means He could have refused to go. Once you understand that, it adds a whole new perspective to the dark night He endured in the Garden of Gethsemane. I believe God also takes risks with us. We too have free will. We can use that freedom to honour or dishonour Jesus. We can use it to serve Him or serve ourselves with the gifts, time and money that He has given us. It also follows, since we were made in His image (Gen. 1:27), that we were made to have the capacity to take risks as well. Some of us are of course more risk averse than others but let me put this to you: taking a risk isn't ungodly or counter to the gospel. Obviously it depends on the kind of risks we are taking, but here are a couple of questions to ask yourself to see if you are taking any kingdom-friendly risks: Are you living your life on the edge for Jesus? When was the last time you really entered into a deliberate and stretching adventure of trust? Life's short, with no rehearsal time, so let's all make our time count. Jesus said in Gethsemane that He came to do the will of His Father in heaven and not His own. I wonder what the world would look like if all believers lived like that.

Prayer: Thank You, Father, that Jesus took such an incredibly tough and costly decision to do Your will. Help me to live that way too. Stretch my faith and protect me from wanting to live a life of safety that steals from me the opportunity to see Your glory and power. Amen.

26/ Pork pies and kingdom living

'Never be lacking in zeal, but keep your spiritual fervour, serving the Lord.' **Romans 12:11**

This isn't a rant against pork pies. I want us to think today about the male plagues of apathy and laziness. I'm not so much talking about the sort of laziness that keeps us on the sofa when we should be up and about doing stuff. I want us to think about spiritual laziness. What does this look like? Well, not practising hospitality and kindness. Being insincere and not making an effort with friendships. Looking after number one rather than those around you. It's being pessimistic, not hopeful, and mean, not generous. Sounds harsh, right? It's not, though. That's just the opposite of the list of qualities you will find in Romans 12.

Becoming and staying spiritually fit is a tough discipline and it requires a fair amount of grit and determination. The thing is, though, spiritual fitness is much like physical fitness. Once you get going, you start to see the benefits. There's a pain barrier to get through but it's really worth it. So audit yourself and ask yourself whether you are spiritually fit or getting a bit lazy. Here's a starter for ten today. Be the first man to apologise and show grace in every situation of conflict. That's the spiritual fitness equivalent of ten press-ups.

Prayer: Make me a man of grace who is first to forgive, first to show grace, first to be kind and who models what it is to be a kingdom man. Amen.

27/ Woodbine Willie

'The LORD is my light and my
salvation – whom shall I fear?
The LORD is the stronghold of
my life – of whom shall I be afraid?'
Psalm 27:1

Geoffrey Anketell Studdert Kennedy was an
Anglican vicar and military chaplain in World War I.
He's perhaps better known as Woodbine Willie.
He got his nickname for handing out cigarettes to
the wounded and dying on the battlefields of the
western front. He actually earned a Military Cross
for running into no-man's-land during an attack
on the German trenches so that he could attend
to the dying despite being unarmed and therefore
unable to defend himself. In fact, five military
chaplains have been awarded the Victoria Cross,
Britain's highest award for gallantry for selfless
acts of heroism and sacrifice.

These guys knew it, and King David knew it. As
men of God, who know that Jesus is our captain
and rescuer, we can live life with a bold and

gritty assurance that whatever happens, and no matter how tough things get, it is well with our souls. That's how Woodbine Willie could face the bullets with only a Bible, a prayer and a packet of Woodbines.

Prayer: Grant me courage and boldness, in Jesus' name, to face down the things that I fear and conquer the enemies that make me cower. Amen.

28/Besieged?

'Though an army besiege me, my heart will not fear; though war break out against me, even then will I be confident.' **Psalm 27:3**

My eyes focus on the word 'besiege' when I read this verse. It must be terrifying to face a military besiegement. Cut off with no supplies and help, knowing that a vicious enemy is waiting until you are so weak that you can no longer resist his attack. Imagine it, day after day living in the knowledge that their plan is to snuff you out and take everything from you. Now, I'm pretty much sure that none of us will face that kind of situation physically. I'm more than certain, however, that we will feel spiritually and emotionally besieged at various points in our lives.

The trigger can come from a variety of directions: work hassles, family stresses, financial pressure ... King David faced periods of time when his life was under threat, living in hiding with armies hunting him down. He knew, however, that

God was God. It didn't just make him feel cosy and hugged; rather it allowed him to live with confidence. That's not to be confused with arrogance. Arrogance is an unchecked ego. Confidence in God is assurance that you are not alone in whatever you face, and that's priceless.

Prayer: Whenever I feel pressured from every side, remind me, Holy Spirit, that I can stay confident because You are with me. Amen.

29/ Sometimes you've just got to go through it

'Hear my voice when I call, LORD;
be merciful to me and answer me.'
Psalm 27:7

Sometimes when you are in the thick of it, it's easy to feel alone. More than that, you can begin to feel that God has forgotten you as well. I guess in this particular psalm, where enemies surrounded David, he was feeling pretty afraid and really needed to know that God was with Him. It's at times like that when we need to remember some solid foundational stuff. The Bible says categorically that God will never leave or forsake us. You'll find that in Hebrews 13:5.

I am reminded of the stories of the Israelites, when they would cry out to God to rescue them. The Bible shows us time and time again that He heard them. It's just that sometimes He lets us go through stuff to shape us and mould us. In some cases in the Bible it took decades! I'm not suggesting it will be the same for you. What I am saying is that sometimes we need to remember that we serve a God who doesn't 'do a runner'. He's heard you. Now you need to get some grit, remember the truth and crack on.

Prayer: Lord, grant to me a bit of grit, determination and courage to hold the line in the moments when I feel alone. I choose to believe Your Word, which tells me that I am never alone. Amen.

30/The ending's a good one

'I remain confident of this: I will see the goodness of the LORD in the land of the living. Wait for the LORD; be strong and take heart and wait for the LORD.' **Psalm 27:13-14**

Here's a rock-solid Bible fact: the Gospels have a happy ending. We know just by skipping to the last page of the Bible that one day, despite all the challenges, ups, downs, trials, tribulations, heart-aches, bruises and scars that it's all going to be all right!

However, we also have to face the reality that sometimes it's hard to believe that the good news on the last page applies to us! There will be blokes all over the place reading this today who are facing a tough time. It might be that you are one of them. If that's the case, the message from the psalm is simple: 'be strong and take heart.' I think in those moments of despair that we have to decide to take a deep breath, get our heads straight and make a decision to keep looking up. It's tough but it's better than the alternative of looking at the ground through a filter of despair. It's when we decide to look up at Jesus that He is able to walk with us through the storm.

Prayer: I will keep looking up at You, Jesus, and today I choose to walk forward in the confident hope that I will see Your goodness in this life as well as the next. Amen.

31/ Embrace the desert

'Jesus, full of the Holy Spirit, left the Jordan and was led by the Spirit into the wilderness.' **Luke 4:1**

I once went on an expedition that lasted 21 days. I was 18 at the time and, as part of it, I had to spend 48 hours on my own in a forest on the edge of Snowdonia. I had to make myself a shelter and only had water and a few snacks to keep me going. At the time it was a tough challenge, but I remember feeling like a new man at the end of it. I think in many ways it gave me a real maturity boost.

Wilderness, or so-called desert, experiences can actually be really good for us. Jesus, at the start of His ministry, was strengthened in His resolve in the wilderness. The devil certainly attacked Him there and would of course continue to do so. But it's clear that the Holy Spirit was the One who was leading Jesus into the wilderness for good reason. Perhaps it was a master class in how the devil would seek to tempt Him in the years ahead.

In the same way, we shouldn't always see our own wilderness experiences as totally negative times. It's in these moments that we can grow in strength and purpose. In fact, I would go so far as to say that us men need desert times. If it was good enough for Moses (who spent about 40 years tending sheep after committing murder before he became a leader for 40 years in the desert) then it's good enough for me. One thing I have found is that a wilderness experience usually precedes God asking me to do something (if I embrace the desert challenge, that is). That's certainly true in the Bible too and I've no doubt that God uses such times extensively to fashion and shape us for the task ahead.

Prayer: Lord, I accept that there will be times in my life that will feel like I am in the wilderness spiritually. In those times fashion me, break me and mould me so that I might be more useful to You and Your purposes. Amen.

32/Fight back

'The devil said to him, "If you are the son of God, tell this stone to become bread." Jesus answered, "It is written: 'Man shall not live on bread alone.'"' **Luke 4:3-4**

Notice that Jesus went to war against the devil's temptations. His battle plan was simple. He didn't shout, yell, stamp his feet or bang a drum. He simply quoted Scripture in reply to every temptation. I like that. Jesus quoted from Deuteronomy every time the devil came at Him. In fact it was so effective that, at one point in the exchange, the devil quotes from Psalm 91 in an attempt to play Him at His own game. Jesus of course just came straight back at him.

This is a simple reminder for us men today that the Word of God has power to resist the enemy. Therefore we would do well to work hard at getting it under our skin. Let's face it, most men don't like to read and for the most part we're not good at spiritual disciplines. This, however, is worth working at.

Next time you feel tempted, be ready with a reply from the Bible. It might just save your bacon.

Prayer: Inspire me to get to grips with Your Word, help me to remember verses when I read them and to store in my head and my heart truth from Scripture that will overcome temptations when they are fired in my direction. Amen.

33/Watch your back

'When the devil had finished all this tempting, he left him until an opportune time.' **Luke 4:13**

It's easy to miss this verse and yet it's there right at the end of the temptation in the desert story. Luke is the only Gospel account that includes this line but I believe it's so important. What it tells us is that, although Jesus had successfully fought off the enemy's attack, it was just one round of the battle (and certainly not the first or the last).

The enemy, it seems, is a persistent foe and we would do well to remember that fact. I'm not saying we should live in superstitious fear of the enemy. Far from it. In fact I think the reverse and I'm the first to say that we give him far too much time and attention. It just means that we need to stay vigilant. Keep your spiritual wits about you at all times.

Spend a moment now, just a brief moment, asking the Holy Spirit if there are any chinks in your armour, or any areas in your life where you are particularly vulnerable. If anything comes to mind, tell some mates and get it sorted. If you don't, you yourself will be vulnerable as the enemy spies his 'opportune time' for your life.

Prayer: Keep me wise to the attacks of the enemy and keep me vigilant in the areas of my life where I am weakest. Amen.

34/Radical

'The Spirit of the Lord is on me, because he has anointed me to proclaim good news to the poor.'
Luke 4:18

This is how Jesus begins His public ministry. He doesn't do it with a ten-point action plan or a trendy slogan. He does it by again quoting Scripture (this time Isaiah) and by making His intention absolutely clear. He had come to minister to the bust-up people. Yes, He did come for everyone but you can't ignore the fact that by making the opening words of His public ministry orientated towards the poor, the captive and the blind He was making a significant point that He wanted us to hear.

The big question we all need to ask, however, is in what ways are we as men living out Luke 4:18 in our own lives? Do you communicate the good news? Do you mix solely with like-minded people, or are you reaching out to the people the world sees as 'losers'? Men have a reputation for being cynical and untrusting. It gives a clear message to the world that there are some transformed men around when we start to live our own lives a different way.

Pray: Holy Spirit, anoint me and help me to be a man of good news to people who do not know You. Help me to reach out to people at work/college or at home who I wouldn't normally mix with. Amen.

And as I've gotten older, I've had more of a tendency to look for people who live by kindness, tolerance, compassion, a gentler way of looking at things.

MARTIN SCORSESE

35/Known in hell

> "'Go away! What do you want with us, Jesus of Nazareth? Have you come to destroy us? I know who you are – the Holy One of God!'"
>
> **Luke 4:34**

There's a similar account to this in Acts 19:13-16 where the sons of a Jewish chief priest were trying to cast out demons in 'the name of Jesus, whom Paul preaches'. In that case the demon replies that it knows who Paul is and who Jesus is but not who they are! The men get a beating as a result! Both Jesus and Paul the apostle had a reputation in hell; the men, however, were unknown. When you gave your life to Christ you too became known in hell. To become a follower of Jesus is to make an open declaration of war against the forces of darkness. You became, in many senses, a marked man. The tragedy is, of course, that many men who follow Jesus have a reputation in hell for all the wrong reasons. Today then is simply about asking an honest question and facing up to the answer: as a man of God, what do you think your reputation in hell is for?

If the answer isn't a good one, don't despair. Just talk to some mates, pray the issues through, make good whatever needs to be put right and get back into the fight.

Prayer: May my life be used for Your glory and not the devil's. May my steps be on the narrow path and my skills and gifts used to fight the good fight and to see Jesus glorified. Amen.

36/ Jesus and a scumbag

'While Jesus was in one of the towns, a man came along who was covered with leprosy. When he saw Jesus, he fell with his face to the ground and begged him, "Lord, if you are willing, you can make me clean."' **Luke 5:12**

The guy with leprosy was understandably desperate. He was a social outcast and seen as spiritually as well as physically unclean. To put it bluntly, the world saw him as scum. He knew his need and he also knew that Jesus was his only hope. It was that desperation that put him on his knees, face to the ground.

As men we can suffer with a tremendously toxic condition called 'self-sufficiency'. We love to think that we are totally capable and in no need of a crutch. If we show our need in front of others we worry that it will be seen as weakness. We don't make ourselves vulnerable for similar reasons. The thing is, we are all totally dependent on God. As I read this passage I found myself being challenged to think: when was the last time I was on my knees before God? When was the last time I acknowledged my total dependency on Him? Why wait until the chips are down to do that? Perhaps today we all need to find a quiet moment in a private space and spend some time with our faces lowered to the ground before the King of kings.

We also see Jesus here touching someone no one else would touch. We don't see lepers as 'scum' today, but we also aren't likely to encounter a sufferer. We are, however, called to be Jesus to the outcast and the marginalised. Who might Jesus be challenging you to reach out to?

Prayer: Heavenly Father, I acknowledge my total dependence on You. You are the giver of life, the sustainer of the universe. I surrender my life again to You. In Jesus' name. Amen.

37/Quiet places

'But Jesus often withdrew to lonely places and prayed.' **Luke 5:16**

Everyone's busy, right? Talk to the average bloke and within a few minutes he'll tell you he is busy. Look around at the people in their cars, on the train or walking down the street and you'll see that they all look under pressure. It's the way of the world today. Jesus knew what busy was, with crowds clamouring around Him wherever He went, debates with religious leaders, demands on Him for His time and pressure from all sides. How did He cope as a man? Simple, He withdrew. Sometimes we just have to do that for our own sanity. Sometimes we have to say 'no' to the demands placed upon us and withdraw to a quiet place to get our heads together and, most importantly, to remind ourselves what life is really all about. We need to make sure that we are in contact with God and that our relationship with Him is strong. It's in the quiet place that we so often hear God speak. Yes, He talks to us in the busyness as well but it is much harder to hear

Him so we simply must make time to cut out the clutter. Perhaps you need to look at your diary and factor some quiet time in? Perhaps you need to cancel some stuff to make sure it happens. One thing's for sure, if it was important to Jesus, it's absolutely crucial for us if we are to finish the race well.

Prayer: Heavenly Father, I submit my busy life to You, along with my plans and schedules. I am sorry for time that I have stolen from You and sorry for the times when I have gone silent and not made the time to listen to You. Amen.

[REBUILD]

38/ Prayer and action – an explosive combination

'They said to me, "Those who survived the exile and are back in the province are in great trouble and disgrace. The wall of Jerusalem is broken down, and its gates have been burned with fire." When I heard these things, I sat down and wept. For some days I mourned and fasted and prayed before the God of heaven.' **Nehemiah 1:3-4**

Here Nehemiah, the cupbearer to the king, gets some pretty bad news. His is an interesting response. If you are anything like me, when I'm faced with a crisis or a challenge I go straight into 'fix-it mode'. Everything in me wants to put it right, provide a solution, dash to the rescue or come up with a strategic plan. That's not what Nehemiah does though, is it? The first thing he does is to get on his knees and pray. More than that, he prayed with a broken heart. Even more than that, he fasted. There's hidden power in prayer and fasting, of that I have no doubt. The problem is us men tend to jump into action without the pause in the quiet first. It's when we pause to listen or to seek God's best way forward that we find a straighter path. I'm reminded of Proverbs 16:3, which says our success comes from placing our plans before the Lord. We would do well to do that.

Note that Nehemiah not only prayed but fasted too! That can be a very neglected discipline today but I'm sure it's where a lot of hidden spiritual power can be found. There's plenty of teaching out there about fasting and some sensible advice but, in short, why not miss a meal today and commit to pray for something or someone when you would otherwise be eating?

Prayer: I commit to You, Heavenly Father, my plans, thoughts and ideas, strategies and solutions. Show me a better way if there is one and give me success when my plans and ideas please You. Amen.

39/ Where does success come from?

'Then I said to them, "You see the trouble we are in: Jerusalem lies in ruins, and its gates have been burned with fire. Come, let us rebuild the wall of Jerusalem and we will no longer be in disgrace ... The God of heaven will give us success."' **Nehemiah 2:17,20a**

Nehemiah faced an absolutely mammoth task. With just a ragtag group of exiles he was attempting to rebuild Jerusalem's walls with huge stones while surrounded by enemies. His utter faith in his ability to get the job done could come across as arrogance, but it wasn't. He knew God had called him to the task and that it was He who would give them success. He didn't see God as a crutch, he saw Him as the provider of his strength. That's different.

I remember when I landed my first job in London as a salesman for a bank. It had been a long and involved interview process and I was one of the few people to land a job in quite a lucrative role. I was quite full of myself, but then someone at church made a throwaway comment along the lines of 'you know who to thank, don't you?' I felt really indignant. After all it was me who had passed the interview, who had the gifts and ability. How arrogant! It was only years later that I started to really understand that it is God who grants success and God who is there when we fail. Lean not on your own understanding, fellas, or on your ability. God is the provider – not you.

Prayer: I acknowledge that all I have and all that I am and will be is only because of Your grace. Thank You for the success You give me and thank You for being there when I hit the wall. I owe You everything and I commit all that I am and all that I have to You. Amen.

40/All hands on deck

'Uzziel son of Harhaiah, one of the goldsmiths, repaired the next section; and Hananiah, one of the perfume-makers, made repairs next to that. They restored Jerusalem as far as the Broad Wall ... Shallum son of Hallohesh, ruler of a half-district of Jerusalem, repaired the next section with the help of his daughters.' **Nehemiah 3:8,12**

I love this scripture. There's a job to do and just about everybody gets stuck in. It's incredible – there are perfume-makers and daughters all shoulder to shoulder rebuilding the walls. This is a salutary reminder to us that we need to do things as a team if we are to accomplish great things for God. Great though the *Rambo* and *Rocky* movies are, I don't think we were ever meant to be super solo soldiers. We were designed to be in a band of brothers who support each other, and rub the rough edges off one another as iron sharpens iron.

The thing I love about this passage is the unlikely characters involved. Perfume-makers laying bricks? Daughters shovelling sand? I love it! What a picture! It also says to me that at times we need to get stuck in doing things we don't instinctively enjoy in order to help each other out.

Prayer: I will stand by my brothers when they need me to get stuck in and I will call for help when I need them to stand with me. As iron sharpens iron so I will journey with the men around me as we seek to serve Jesus. In Your name I pray. Amen.

41/Expect opposition

'When Sanballat heard that we were rebuilding the wall, he became angry and was greatly incensed. He ridiculed the Jews.'
Nehemiah 4:1

It's a certain truth, and one that I have seen proved over and over again. Determine to do something for God, great or small, and you will face opposition. It's just the way it is. So if you are a man who wants to get active for God, take note of this now. If you are already active for God, I've just explained why sometimes people seem to oppose you even though you are just trying to serve the kingdom.

I think that sometimes we forget that there is a war on out there. There are two kingdoms clashing and when you determine to stand for Jesus, you in effect make a declaration of war against the forces of darkness. You become a marked man. So stand firm and don't quit. Don't give in to the small voice of doubt niggling away in the background or the weight of pressure suddenly upon you. Opposition is a sure sign that you are on the right track.

Prayer: Lord, give me the peace of Your presence and the strength and will to fight through obstructions and discouragement to stand strong. Amen.

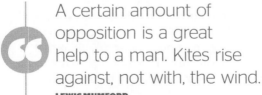

A certain amount of opposition is a great help to a man. Kites rise against, not with, the wind.

LEWIS MUMFORD

42/ Persevering while under attack

'After I looked things over, I stood up and said to the nobles, the officials and the rest of the people, "Don't be afraid of them. Remember the Lord, who is great and awesome, and fight for your families, your sons and your daughters, your wives and your homes."' Nehemiah 4:14

This passage shows Nehemiah going into combat mode. Immediately after his declaration the people listening pick up their spears and start work, sharing the burden of guarding the area too. They used spears and swords for some of the day and shovels and trowels for the rest. This was full-on stuff. They were under genuine threat but kept on going. I sometimes think that the Church has gone a bit passive. We've got so into the theology of the 'open door' that at the slightest bit of opposition we chuck the towel in, or start to think that maybe the Lord is sending us a sign that He is closing the door to the idea or plan. Sometimes that may be true, but I think in the majority of cases that's rubbish, so now it takes far more than a couple of obstructions to persuade me that God is telling me to stop. Sometimes you will have to go into combat mode too and understand that not everything is going to be plain sailing when you are doing things for God. Do as Nehemiah did – remember the Lord, remember who or what you are standing for and crack on!

Prayer: I determine to fight for the gospel and not quit at the slightest problem. I remember that You are the greatest and I will stand up for justice and truth even in the face of opposition. Amen.

43/ Bust a gut

'So we continued the work with half the men holding spears, from the first light of dawn till the stars came out. At that time I also said to the people, "Let every man and his helper stay inside Jerusalem at night, so that they can serve us as guards by night and as workers by day."' **Nehemiah 4:21-22**

In an increasingly busy world, it's not uncommon to hear people talking about 'work/life balance' and the need to ensure that plenty of time is taken for rest and play. It's hugely unfashionable now to talk about working extra hours. Yet here we see Nehemiah clearly calling people to an almost 24/7 working pattern! So what do we take from this? It seems clear to me that there will be seasons in our lives when it's both necessary and right to put in an extra shift and bust a gut. These were special times for Nehemiah and his men. They needed to get the job done fast and so they needed to max out and go for broke. I don't think you can or should do this all the time, but we should all be prepared to go the extra mile when it's required.

Practically speaking, there are loads of times when I would rather just stay in bed than get up and run a Sunday School meeting, or put my feet up and watch TV rather than go to a church meeting about some project or other. Perhaps at times like that we all need to remember Nehemiah and his crew. There are certainly times when we need to take a deep breath, grit our teeth and get busy. Sometimes instead of getting stressed over trying to be balanced and failing dismally, we need to realise that there are seasons when we need to put in an extra burst of activity, and just get on with it. Do not, however, work until you completely burn out! Make sure you stay accountable and remember that life is a team effort.

Prayer: God of the working day and the night, help me not to miss opportunities to serve and go the extra distance when it is required. Amen.

44/Where does your strength come from?

'Nehemiah said, "Go and enjoy choice food and sweet drinks, and send some to those who have nothing prepared. This day is holy to our Lord. Do not grieve, for the joy of the LORD is your strength."'

`Nehemiah 8:10`

Nehemiah and the people rebuilt the walls in an astonishing 52 days. Ezra then stood up where everyone could see him and read the book of the Law. The Bible tells us that as the people heard God's Word being read to them, they broke down in tears. What comes next isn't perhaps what you would expect. Nehemiah essentially told them to throw a party! The explanation is simple – your strength comes from feeling pretty great about knowing God! It's worth remembering that. We seem to live in an increasingly miserable culture. Listen in on conversations and so many of them involve the language of complaint. Everybody's whinging and moaning. We, however, are the redeemed and we know Jesus. Surely that means we should have a different outlook and a different perspective. It's definitely worth remembering that next time you are caught in traffic! Keep joyful and keep in the Word. That's where your true strength lies.

Prayer: My joy and my strength are found in You, Lord. I will remember that truth in the good times and the bad times. I will praise You in all circumstances for my hope is in You. Amen.

[KNOWN]

45/ Is there anybody out there?

'You have searched me, LORD, and you know me. You know when I sit and when I rise; you perceive my thoughts from afar.' **Psalm 139:1-2**

Being a bit of a Pink Floyd fan, as I read the start of what is an amazing psalm, I was reminded of one of the tracks on the album *The Wall*, which asks the question, 'is there anybody out there?' This psalm more than answers that question. It tells us that not only is God out there but He knows you completely; right down to the detail of when you sit and stand. More than that, He knows your thoughts as well. I find this incredible.

I don't know what life holds for you as you read this today – things could be great or they could be pretty rubbish. Some of you may be feeling desperate. Be assured as we read through this psalm over the next few days that you aren't on your own. Though at times it may feel like it, the truth is that we follow a God who not only made us but He searches us and knows us right down to the smallest detail ... and He still wants to know us! That's grace – isn't it amazing?

Prayer: Thank You, Father, for Your presence. Thank You that I am not alone but that You search me and know me. Help me to understand that in an ever deeper way. Amen.

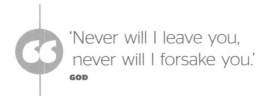

'Never will I leave you, never will I forsake you.'
GOD

46/Say what?

'You discern my going out and my lying down; you are familiar with all my ways. Before a word is on my tongue you, LORD, know it completely.' **Psalm 139:3-4**

Is this for real? So before any of us says anything, God knows what is going to come out of our mouths? It would seem so if we are to believe what the Bible says. I think that has profound implications for us men. I don't know about you, but just taking a moment to think about this has made me ponder on the things I say. You might feel you can get away with saying some things angrily or negatively to people ... but are you happy that God knows that you say those things? Probably not! It's a good reminder for us all today to watch our tongues. God not only hears it all, He knows your heart and what you are going to say even before you do!

What I'm certainly not trying to get you to picture here is an image of God as some kind of cosmic

Big-Brother-style thought policeman. I don't think fear is a good motivator for any of us. The reading, however, *is* a timely reminder that we are truly living out our lives for an audience of one. I don't know if you have ever had one of those absolutely awful heart-thumping moments when you were whinging or moaning about someone, only to realise they were standing behind you? I guess that's partly what I picture here. So be concerned for what God sees in your head and in your heart. Thinking about this again makes me want to audit and check myself a bit more – how about you?

Prayer: Help me, God, to speak words of life and not death, nothing more and nothing less. Amen.

47/Get some perspective

'You hem me in behind and before, and you lay your hand upon me. Such knowledge is too wonderful for me, too lofty for me to attain.'
Psalm 139:5-6

As I ponder on these verses I feel really challenged. Being a bloke, I love to think of myself as all-capable, all-sufficient and certainly in no need of a crutch. Don't get me wrong. I can act humble, I can project being humble and I can do humble things ... but how often do I consciously acknowledge that there is not only a limit to my ability but there is One who is so much greater than I am? One who is so awesome that I can't even get a handle on His greatness?

In several of the psalms, it says 'your greatness, no one can fathom ...' That phrase really stirs and moves me. It puts me in my place and gives me a healthy perspective on my life and my hopes and ambitions. Who is each one of us compared to the Lord? It's good for each of us as men to humble ourselves. Pondering the greatness of God and realising it is beyond our comprehension is certainly a good starting place!

Prayer: You, God, have all the power and all the glory. I cannot even comprehend the extent of Your glory and majesty. Thank You that despite this I am still Your son. Amen.

48/Nowhere to run to ...

'Where can I go from your Spirit? Where can I flee from your presence? If I go up to the heavens, you are there; if I make my bed in the depths, you are there.'
Psalm 139:7-8

You can't get away from God. Fact. There is nowhere you can go to escape Him. Fact. You can't outrun Him and you can't dodge Him. Fact. Listen up: there is no desert or valley experience that you can go through that will put you out of His reach. Sometimes you might want to 'do a runner' and sometimes you may just want to hide yourself away but it will be a pointless exercise. God knows you, loves you unconditionally as a son and does so with a persistent determination. Sometimes, that's all we need to know. Sometimes that's just about all we can take in. This is a kind of 'back-pocket truth' for a tough time. It's knowledge about God that you need to draw on when the day comes (and it most certainly will) when you find yourself in a tough place.

I can remember one time in my early twenties feeling close to the edge with stress over a few really tough issues. Everything in me wanted to chuck in the towel and crawl under a rock somewhere ... It was in that still moment of despair, with everything crowding in, that I felt God say to me: 'remember, you were worth dying for, son ...' Priceless. Even in what was a self-inflicted dark place, God was there.

Prayer: I acknowledge that You are the God of 'everywhere'. Thank You that You are everywhere I find myself, even when I'm in the darkest places – and even when I'm trying to run away! Amen.

49/Gripped and guided

'If I rise on the wings of the dawn, if I settle on the far side of the sea, even there your hand will guide me, your right hand will hold me fast.' **Psalm 139:9-10**

There's a big difference between being directed and being guided. When we are directed, we have no choice. The path is mapped out and we can't deviate. When we are guided, we are shown the best route forward but our free will means we can make a choice to go with it or not! If we ensure we spend time listening to the voice of the Holy Spirit and read God's Word, then we can be confident that our steps are being guided by Him. The thing is, however, that we can do all these things and still find ourselves feeling stretched, challenged and in unexpected places.

That's where faith comes in and the previous years of building a solid relationship with God will help us stand in such times. It is out of such a strong and functioning relationship with God that we can be assured that we are in His grip. The verses above say that we are being held fast. To me that means that even in the midst of the most ferocious storm I can stand my ground because there is One who is far greater than me, holding me in place.

Prayer: Thank You for Your guiding hand and thank You that I am in Your grip. Thank You that this is true, even when I don't feel it! Thank You for the confidence and strength that this truth gives me. Amen.

50/Knitting?!?

'For you created my inmost being; you knit me together in my mother's womb. I praise you because I am fearfully and wonderfully made; your works are wonderful, I know that full well.'
Psalm 139:13-14

I guess you weren't expecting to see the word 'knit' in a men's devotional book (despite it being a truly manly pastime in yesteryear!). But that's just how the Bible says you were put together. I believe it's saying that God was involved in every process of you coming into existence, right down to the smallest, most intricate detail.

I'm a big fan of motorsport and can spend hours looking at the engineering involved in putting together a high performance machine. The detail and technology is off the scale! The same applies to you. Now, you may not believe this when you look in the mirror in the mornings but this verse is saying that you are wonderfully made. The thrust of this is that you are valuable as a person, not just as a machine or workhorse. To God your life is of significance. You weren't an accident and nor are you a spare part. Your life has meaning to God. Once each one of us starts to live a life in response to this truth, the results will be explosive and will change the way we view ourselves and others.

Prayer: Help me to see myself as You see me, God. Help me to live a life that is an appropriate response to the care and attention You gave me when You planned it. I praise You today for the truth that I am fearfully and wonderfully made. Amen.

51/Men wear masks

'Search me, God, and know my heart; test me and know my anxious thoughts.' **Psalm 139:23**

Anxiety – now there's a secret male issue. As blokes we don't find it easy to share what's really going on in our lives. We can find it really tough to be vulnerable and let some other guys know that in reality we're struggling a bit. So instead we wear masks. We would so often rather project to everyone that all is well. We are so good at the mask-wearing lark that we can even kid ourselves that all is well! That is, until we suddenly blow up or burn out.

The starting point for changing this is perhaps what we find in the psalm. We may not be able to be instantly honest with our mates about how we are doing, but we can be honest with God. Can't we? It's a good discipline to regularly say to God, 'search my heart and know my anxious thoughts'. Once you are used to being honest with God you'll probably find the courage to seek out a few mates and ask them to pray with you. I make sure there are a few guys I see regularly so that we can all support each other through thick and thin and respond to what we feel God is saying. After all, no man is an island!

Prayer: In the quietness of this moment, search my heart and know my anxious thoughts. Please give me Your peace and give me the guts to talk to my mates when I need to. At the same time, please show me how and when to be there for my mates who might be struggling in the times when I am not. Amen.

52/A gutsy question

'See if there is any offensive way in me, and lead me in the way everlasting.' **Psalm 139:24**

It takes a courageous man to ask this question. It also takes honesty and the guts to face up to the answer. We all have our blind spots, don't we? And by definition they can be hard to spot! I have some close friends and a great wife, Karen, who all let me know about my blind spots – but it can be tremendously painful when they do! However, I'm grateful that they do let me know, despite the angst and the instant indignation that seems to well up inside me! I want to be the kind of man that I know I ought to be and, in all honesty, in order to get there I know I have to go through the pain barrier. But it's not just our mates and people very close to us we should rely on. It's only God, as this psalm has shown us, who knows us inside out. It's only God who knows everything about us.

So ask God how you are really doing and you might get a tough reply. It'll be worth it though. You can be assured of that. He just wants you to be the best that you can be – for yourself, but also for Him, so that people will see His Son, Jesus, shining through the example and conduct of your life.

Prayer: Search me, God, test me and examine my heart. Please let me know what it is about my life and attitude that offends You and show me what I need to do in order to straighten it out. Amen.

[ATTITUDE BEATITUDES]

53/Get bitter

'You are the salt of the earth.'
Matthew 5:13

In the days before fridges, to prevent a maggot infestation in meat people rubbed salt into the flesh. The deeper the salt went, the more likely they were to retard the decay and stop the rot. That's exactly what we're meant to be doing in the world today! It drives me insane that I keep hearing people reinforcing the Christian ghetto. How often have you heard these phrases: 'I know a good Christian accountant', 'my mechanic's a Christian' or, even worse, 'my barber's a Christian'? Why have Christians got obsessed about only using Christians? Get out there and get involved with the world and be the salt Jesus told us we are! Be a rot-delayer and a decay-defeater. Yes, it may result in you finding yourself having to face tough situations, but if you aren't in the places where you can smell the rot you're not involved enough! It was never meant to be easy to follow Jesus. In fact, the normal state for a believer is to find himself being challenged.

If you're normally comfortable and secure, just maybe something is wrong?

Prayer: Heavenly Father, show me the places where I need to go in order to stop the rot. Show me how to get involved in retarding decay. Help me not to moan about the world but to help change it! Amen.

We should not ask, 'What is wrong with the world?' for that diagnosis has already been given. Rather, we should ask, 'What has happened to the salt and light?'

JOHN R. W. STOTT

54/Halogen believers

'You are the light of the world. A town built on a hill cannot be hidden.' **Matthew 5:14**

A group of guys I know had just formed a new Bible study group and decided to meet in a coffee shop first thing in the morning. A classic scenario followed. There was loads of background noise, right until the moment when my mate, who was leading the group, decided to go for it and open in prayer. He told me that at that precise moment everyone in the café stopped talking and all the kitchen noise stopped. Basically everyone tuned in on his prayer across the whole floor of the café. OK, so he may have felt like he wanted the ground to swallow him up but I really like that scenario. We were never meant to be ninjas, hidden and undercover. After all, what have we got to be ashamed of? Do people at work know what you stand for? Do people know you follow Jesus? If you were to tell them, would it make sense to them because they've already seen the witness of your character – or would it be a shock? We weren't meant to be like tea lights; rather 500-watt halogen lamps – and then some. So get out there and let your light shine. Just don't be weird with it and get a reputation for ramming your beliefs down people's throats or being so puritanical you lose all touch with the world we were meant to engage with.

Prayer: Give me the guts to live out my faith publicly. Show me the dark areas in which You want me to shine the light of Jesus and help me to be consistent in the things I say and the things I do. Amen.

55/Toxic lust

> "'You have heard that it was said, 'You shall not commit adultery.' But I tell you that anyone who looks at a woman lustfully has already committed adultery with her in his heart.'" **Matthew 5:27**

Let me just say it as it is. We've got to get brutal with lust. We've got to watch where we look, watch where we go and watch what we fill our heads with. There's so much at stake. In today's passage Jesus takes the Law and ramps it up. The fact is, you can give your heart over to lust on a look and fill your head with sex stuff that's so toxic that it becomes a relationship killer. The thing is, adultery doesn't start at the point where you jump into bed with another woman. It starts a long time before that. It starts by numbing and blunting your conscience and taking the odd, slight wrong turning. Guys, it just ain't worth it.

So get brutal with lust and fight it full on. Be honest with your mates and make a covenant with your eyes not to look where you shouldn't. Let me say this as well: if you are already pretty full on down the path of adultery in your heart, there is grace for you. Don't believe the lie that God's finished with you. Be honest, get real, ask for His grace and forgiveness and get back in the fight.

Prayer: I make a covenant with my eyes. Forgive me where I have gone wrong and make me clean inside again. Purify my thoughts and help me keep on the narrow path. Amen.

56/ Love 'em, don't like 'em?

> "'You have heard that it was said, 'Love your neighbour and hate your enemy.' But I tell you, love your enemies and pray for those who persecute you.'" **Matthew 5:43-44**

Hmm! This is a tough one, so we're going to take a couple of days over it. Firstly, I want to take on the phrase that's often bandied about: 'I love them but I don't like them'. I kind of get that but somehow it just feels a bit cheap. It feels like a two-faced kind of love that gives you permission to still moan about the person concerned or forgive yourself for having the fantasy of putting your boss/mate/neighbour out of the upper floor window of a tower block ... Jesus talks here about praying for people who are persecuting you. I really don't think that Jesus was talking about a 'and dear God please wipe this person out and destroy them by midday today. Amen' type of prayer. I think He was talking about praying for

God to bless them and change their hearts. This can sound a bit much – and it's certainly not the way of the world. But then, we don't live as the world lives, do we? We have a different code to live by. I guess before we can pray for our enemies, then, we need to get our own hearts right, which is what we'll be looking at next time.

Prayer: I know this is a tough one, Father, but help me to have the kind of heart for people that You want me to have, even to the extent of really loving those who are making my life tough. Please start to change me. Amen.

57/Give peace a chance

'He causes his sun to rise on the evil and the good, and sends rain on the righteous and the unrighteous. If you love those who love you, what reward will you get?'
Matthew 5:45-46

It's only God who really knows the condition of our hearts. Look back on the readings we did around Psalm 139 to ponder that awesome truth a bit more. In fact you could take a minute or two if you have your Bible with you and read it again now ... God knows us inside out. He also knows in great detail those who we might like to think are complete scum. Despite this, He still gives us – and them – all we need to live. In other words He gives people a chance. Take it a step further and think about this. He knows what you are really like and He still supplies all you need. Let's face it, if the people around us really knew what went on in our heads and what we were like when no one was looking, it could get pretty uncomfortable. So cut people some slack. Learn to give the benefit of the doubt and believe the best. After all, that's what God keeps doing for you, right? It's called grace.

Prayer: Father, challenge me when I'm not giving the benefit of the doubt or believing the best about someone. Remind me to look at my own life before I judge others. Amen.

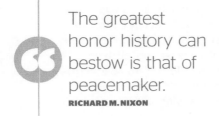

The greatest honor history can bestow is that of peacemaker.
RICHARD M. NIXON

58/Get your head down!

'Do you not know that in a race all the runners run, but only one gets the prize? Run in such a way as to get the prize.' **1 Corinthians 9:24**

I've run a couple of half marathons and the London Marathon. I've also done some mega-stupid distance cycle rides across a few countries. In each of these endurance challenges, I confess that survival was the name of the game. I didn't set my sights on winning the trophy – it felt enough of an achievement just to finish! When it comes to running the faith race, however, that doesn't seem to be enough. Just staggering across the finish line isn't exactly cutting the mustard as far as the Bible sees it. We're being told to go for it, all guns blazing, pushing ourselves so that we skid, not stumble, across the finish line. That means we need to get into training and it means living with a certain amount of pain. OK, so it doesn't sound appealing but why do we whine like sulking teenagers rather than get on with it? No one ever said that following Jesus was easy – or that it is a crutch. So let's get our heads down and get training. God protect us from mediocrity and passivity!

Prayer: I determine that I will run the race of faith with all my heart, soul and strength. I determine to put in the effort and energy required, not just to stumble through life but to run strong and run fast for Jesus' sake and for His fame and glory. Amen.

59/No pain no gain

'Everyone who competes in the games goes into strict training. They do it to get a crown that will not last, but we do it to get a crown that will last for ever.' **1 Corinthians 9:25**

Having said yesterday that we need to get our heads down and max out, here is the motivation. I guess there will be more than a few blokes reading this today who have got at least one medal or trophy for some kind of sporting endeavour. It's cool to get a medal, and I've got a few scattered around for various different things. The truth is, though, that deep down we known we can't take them with us. The race of faith, however, has eternal consequences and we are told in the verse above that we will one day receive a crown that will last for an eternity.

But just what does the crown represent? I think, in part, it's the people whose lives we have touched. If we run the race of faith hard and fast, then when we cross the finish line we will see some of our mates, family members and/or work colleagues there too. Perhaps they will say to you that they are only there because of you – because you never quit but ran the race in such a way as to win. What a treasure: the crown of those who found Jesus because of you. So get training and get running. There's everything to race for.

Prayer: Father, I keep my eyes on the true prize, a crown that will last for ever. Keep the call of the gospel fixed in my heart and mind and may my life be focused on You and making You known. Amen.

60/Suffer it

'We also glory in our sufferings, because we know that suffering produces perseverance; perseverance, character; and character, hope.' **Romans 5:3-4**

Imagine dying, going to heaven and realising with horror that you are surrounded by a bunch of spoilt brats. What a nightmare that would be! God is in the business of character development in this life and character development can be a painful business. Whatever you do, don't start buying into the rubbish and shallow teaching that tells you that if you come to Christ everything is going to be fantastic. It's just not like that. Bad stuff happens. For example, nine out of the twelve apostles were martyred. Persecution is a constant state of existence for much of the global Church. Now I'm not saying that you will ever face martyrdom or persecution but periods of trial and suffering do go with the territory. It's how we deal with them that matters. God wants to fashion you, mould you, test you, grow you, mature you and

get you ready for an eternity of service. Approach
it in the right way and your hope will grow and
your character will be fashioned ... and perhaps
God will see that He can trust you with more.

**Prayer: Heavenly Father, make
me a man after Your own heart.
Please develop and test me so
that I will be everything that I
can be in Your service. Amen.**

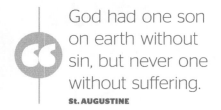

God had one son
on earth without
sin, but never one
without suffering.
St. AUGUSTINE

FIGHTERS/KEEPERS/
LOSERS/REAPERS

More Bible notes for men written by Carl Beech.

Contains:

- 60 daily readings and prayers

- Two guest contributors:
  Roy Crowne & Carl's mate
  Alex Willmott

- Themes to encourage and
  challenge you

'Powerful, personal and relevant'
BEAR GRYLLS

ISBN: 978-1-85345-770-8

Also available in ebook formats

Courses and seminars

Publishing and new media

Conference facilities

Transforming lives

CWR's vision is to enable people to experience personal transformation through applying God's Word to their lives and relationships.

Our Bible-based training and resources help people around the world to:
• Grow in their walk with God
• Understand and apply Scripture to their lives
• Resource themselves and their church
• Develop pastoral care and counselling skills
• Train for leadership
• Strengthen relationships, marriage and family life and much more.

Our insightful writers provide daily Bible-reading notes and other resources for all ages, and our experienced course designers and presenters have gained an international reputation for excellence and effectiveness.

CWR's Training and Conference Centre in Surrey, England, provides excellent facilities in an idyllic setting – ideal for both learning and spiritual refreshment.

CWR Applying God's Word
to everyday life and relationships

CWR, Waverley Abbey House,
Waverley Lane, Farnham,
Surrey GU9 8EP, UK

Telephone: **+44 (0)1252 784700**
Email: **info@cwr.org.uk**
Website: **www.cwr.org.uk**

Registered Charity No 294387
Company Registration No 1990308

it's time for a new kind of man

connecting
men to Jesus
& the church to men

Partner with us
Connect a men's grou
Start a men's group
Join a movement

Equipping and resourcing you to
share Jesus with the men around you

networking || events   resources || training

cvm.org.uk

CVM is a movement that offers a range of advice,
resources and men's events across the UK and be
The Hub, Unit 2, Dunston Rd, Chesterfield S41 8XA Tel: 01246
Registered Charity in England & Wales (No.1071663)
A Company Ltd by Guarantee (No.3623498)